Jemima is the founder of
Stress Free Life Academy.

Dedicated to sharing the power of practical and effective techniques to transform your life.

This is a book based on her 100 stress free days series on instagram.

#100stressfreedays

@stressfreelifeacademy

www.stressfreelifeacademy.com

Happy de-stressing!
with love,
Jemima
xx

Dearest Emma,
to help with your self-soothing
H ♥ x

Publication May 2022.

© Stress Free Life Academy

All rights reserved.

The right of Jemima Blazdell to be identified as author of this work has been asserted in accordance with Section 77 of the Copyright, Designs and Patents Act 1988

Thanks to:

Ally Berry for the photography.
Sarah Jeffs of brightfeather.studio for the artwork, diagrams and book design.
Amanda Mannix for proofreading and support.
Laura Prudence for the calligraphy.
Jane Eastwood for the massage.

Kevin Fitzgerald, Cathryn Lavery, Green Chameleon, Alex Litvin, Diego PH and Erica Marsland Huynh on the Unsplash platform for providing the 5 images I needed to complete the book.

100 STRESS FREE DAYS

JEMIMA BLAZDELL

For Jacob.

Thank you for being my brilliant son.

You have no idea how brightly you shine.

100 Stress Free Days

On March 4th 2021 - my 45th birthday - I started a commitment to post a video every day for 100 days on Instagram. It was inspired by the #100happydays project that I had seen and participated in, where you posted a photo that made you happy every day for 100 days.

It seemed like such a simple thing to do. I'm always looking for ways to help people and this felt right. I had the inspiration, sat down and wrote 100 ideas: boom - I was off!

I wanted it to be inspiring, spontaneous, fun and most of all, I wanted it to work - to really make a difference to people. And I did it! I recorded and posted a video every day for 100 days and I absolutely loved it.

Each video was under one minute long and gave simple advice on how to de-stress. I had some great feedback so decided to take it a step further and create this book!

How to use this book

Open it each day and spend time with the prompt.

As you use the techniques, you will notice that the more you do them, the less you will need to do them.

You will train your body and mind to choose to relax, to let go, to do what feels good.

And the better you feel, the better you feel. It's a win-win - for you and everyone in your world.

At the back of the book you will find space where you can note your own thoughts and experiences of the techniques.

What did you like, what worked best for you, when might you try it in your life.

If you would like to know more, please visit:

www.stressfreelifeacademy.com @stressfreelifeacademy

Email: jemima@stressfreelifeacademy.com

CONTENTS

100 STRESS FREE DAYS

DAY ONE - Breathe	8
DAY TWO - Tap one round of EFT	10
DAY THREE - Pivoting - Choose the opposite	12
DAY FOUR - Go for a Walk	14
DAY FIVE Women's Day - Reach out to a woman in your life	16
DAY SIX - Tidy one area	18
DAY SEVEN - If you need help, get help	20
DAY EIGHT - Meditation	22
DAY NINE - Set your intention	24
DAY TEN - Finishing things - your to-do list	26
DAY ELEVEN - Connect with someone	28
DAY TWELVE - Tap in the positive	30
DAY THIRTEEN - Tune!	32
DAY FOURTEEN - Take a different view	34
DAY FIFTEEN - Try hypnotherapy	36
DAY SIXTEEN - Do nothing for 5 minutes	38
DAY SEVENTEEN - Get creative	40
DAY EIGHTEEN - Mix it up - Do something differently	42
DAY NINETEEN - Come up with 10 solutions to a problem	44
DAY TWENTY - What's the best advice you've ever been given?	46
DAY TWENTY ONE - Set yourself a health challenge	48
DAY TWENTY TWO - Focus on what makes you happy	50
DAY TWENTY THREE - Have compassion	52
DAY TWENTY FOUR - Find a rainbow	54
DAY TWENTY FIVE - Have a bath	56
DAY TWENTY SIX - Evoke the Learning State	58
DAY TWENTY SEVEN - What's the kindest thing you could say to yourself?	60
DAY TWENTY EIGHT - What advice would you give your younger self?	62
DAY TWENTY NINE - Drink more water	64
DAY THIRTY - If you ran a shop, what would you sell?	66
DAY THIRTY ONE - Walk down a path you've never been down before	68
DAY THIRTY TWO - List your 10 best qualities	70
DAY THIRTY THREE - Focus on your future self	72
DAY THIRTY FOUR - Take one tiny step towards your goal	74
DAY THIRTY FIVE - List all the good things and good people in your life	76
DAY THIRTY SIX - Describe a happy memory	78
DAY THIRTY SEVEN - Stop pushing - What self-care do you need?	80
DAY THIRTY EIGHT - Emergency tapping	82
DAY THIRTY NINE - Get organised	84
DAY FORTY - Make a decision	86
DAY FORTY ONE - Your body language	88
DAY FORTY TWO - Watch your language	90
DAY FORTY THREE - Say "no" if it's a "no"	92
DAY FORTY FOUR - Tense and release	94
DAY FORTY FIVE - Write down your worries and three things you are grateful for	96
DAY FORTY SIX - Good sleep routine	98
DAY FORTY SEVEN - It's OK not to be OK	100
DAY FORTY EIGHT - Procrastination	102
DAY FORTY NINE - Overcome overwhelm	104

DAY FIFTY - Keep going	106
DAY FIFTY ONE - Choose a word for the day - Peace	108
DAY FIFTY TWO - Look around you with fresh eyes	110
DAY FIFTY THREE - Have a nap	112
DAY FIFTY FOUR - Hot & Cold emotions game	114
DAY FIFTY FIVE - Let the Earth support you	116
DAY FIFTY SIX - Respond rather than react	118
DAY FIFTY SEVEN - Havening	120
DAY FIFTY EIGHT - Happy buttons	122
DAY FIFTY NINE - Heartmath Breathing Technique	124
DAY SIXTY - Trust the process	126
DAY SIXTY ONE - Give yourself a break	128
DAY SIXTY TWO - Forgive something from your past	130
DAY SIXTY THREE - List ten things that went well	132
DAY SIXTY FOUR - Eat an apple mindfully	134
DAY SIXTY FIVE - See how far you've come	136
DAY SIXTY SIX - Comfort break	138
DAY SIXTY SEVEN - Morning Pages	140
DAY SIXTY EIGHT - Loving Kindness Meditation	142
DAY SIXTY NINE - White Light Meditation	144
DAY SEVENTY - Silence	146
DAY SEVENTY ONE - Write with your non-dominant hand	148
DAY SEVENTY TWO - Move into the learning zone	150
DAY SEVENTY THREE - What you think is the problem, isn't the problem	152
DAY SEVENTY FOUR - Clear out your old clothes	154
DAY SEVENTY FIVE - What would… do	156
DAY SEVENTY SIX - Act as if	158
DAY SEVENTY SEVEN - 4-7-8 Breathing Technique	160
DAY SEVENTY EIGHT - Listen to your body	162
DAY SEVENTY NINE - Count something	164
DAY EIGHTY - Who needs your help?	166
DAY EIGHTY ONE - Exercise	168
DAY EIGHTY TWO - 'Eat the frog'	170
DAY EIGHTY THREE - Go fast go alone, go far go together	172
DAY EIGHTY FOUR - Projection	174
DAY EIGHTY FIVE - Tap to ground yourself	176
DAY EIGHTY SIX - Laugh!	178
DAY EIGHTY SEVEN - Change your thoughts	180
DAY EIGHTY EIGHT - Plan a surprise for someone	182
DAY EIGHTY NINE - Don't put it off	184
DAY NINETY - Feel your feelings	186
DAY NINETY ONE - Change your environment	188
DAY NINETY TWO - Massage	190
DAY NINETY THREE - Having a fixed outcome	192
DAY NINETY FOUR - Notice your triggers	194
DAY NINETY FIVE - Affirmations	196
DAY NINETY SIX - The miracle question	198
DAY NINETY SEVEN - What is your 'why'?	200
DAY NINETY EIGHT - Commit	202
DAY NINETY NINE - Accountability	204
DAY ONE HUNDRED - Celebrate!	206

NOTES   209

DAY ONE
Breathe

Today's tip is an easy one: you're just going to breathe. You might notice that when you're stressed, you breathe only up in the top part of your chest.

The breath is restricted and you don't use the whole of your lungs.

So, breathe in now and take the breath all the way down, into your tummy.

Take 3 easy, slow breaths, breathing in and out, in and out, in and out.

Notice how you feel.

The more often you do that relaxed, deep breathing, the more quickly you will relax and it will become automatic, and you will breathe that way naturally..

Enjoy and have a great, breath-conscious day!

DAY TWO
Tap one round of EFT

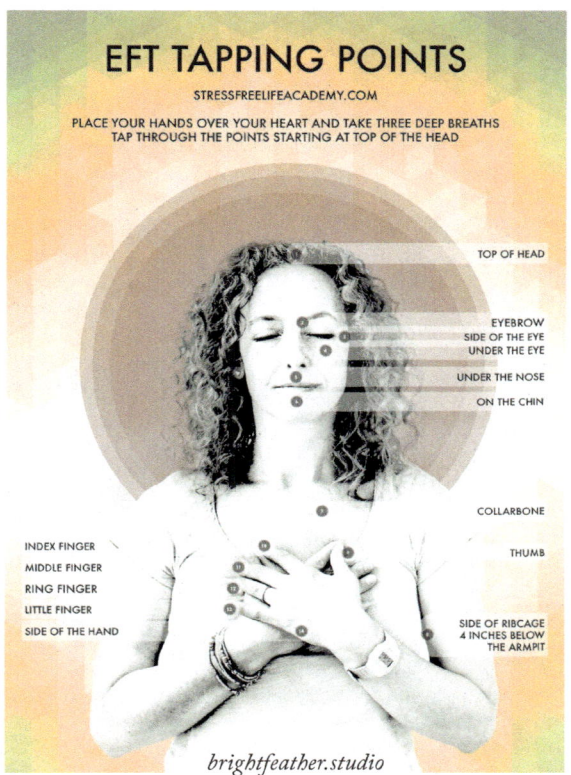

Emotional Freedom Technique is a brilliant tool and today you get to try it out.

Hold your hands over your heart and take an easy, deep breath. Then, take 2 fingers from one hand and start tapping gently on top of your head, and then the beginning of the eyebrow, side of the eye.

Follow the points on the map, gently tapping around 7 times on each point. You've just done one round of EFT – well done!

EFT is also known as 'tapping'. It's used to clear blockages in the body's energy system to help you feel calmer and more relaxed. You can use it to clear stress, emotions and physical sensations from the body. It's so simple: tap through the points and breathe and you will start to notice changes in your body. The more tapping you do, the easier and more effective it becomes.

Go to stressfreelifeacademy.com/freeresources to tap along to a video.

DAY THREE

Pivoting – Choose the opposite

Today's tip is about choosing what you want. It is easy to focus on what you don't want. You might complain that you're cold or that you don't like the situation that you're in and spend a lot of time describing what you don't want and why you don't like it. Maybe you spend a lot of time talking about how bad or difficult things are.

The great news is that when you know what you don't want, you automatically know what you do want. You can start to choose and focus on those things instead. So if you're too cold and you want to be warmer, you can say

"I'm cold, what do I want? To be warmer"
"I'm stressed, I want to be more relaxed."
"I'm unhappy, I want to be happy."

Recognise what you don't want and choose the opposite.

DAY FOUR
Go for a Walk

Getting outside in the fresh air as often as you can helps in lots of ways.

If you're sitting at your desk for a long period of time, or working over a problem or an issue, it can be beneficial to get outside, to blow away the cobwebs and change your energy. You will find ideas and inspirations popping in to your head as you relax and let your mind wander.

If you can't get out for some reason, then open the window or the door and bring some fresh air inside. Move around, shake your body or visualise walking around somewhere in nature that you love. Notice what happens to your body when you shift your attention and choose something else. Enjoy the sunshine and fresh air, wherever you are.

DAY FIVE

Women's Day - Reach out to a woman in your life

This tip was originally recorded on International Women's Day, 8th March 2021. We were in the middle of lockdown and there was still so much uncertainty. It felt really good to acknowledge all the wonderful women who have impacted my life.

Who has impacted your life that you would like to thank?

When you reach out to someone else with gratitude and appreciation, you create connection and community; it helps them and it helps you too.

Send your heart to someone else's now and notice how it feels.

DAY SIX
Tidy one area

You might have noticed that when you have lots going on around you, it can be difficult to settle your mind. This might be true of your external and internal environment.

Have you noticed that when things are more stressful, your house reflects your state of mind? When you're feeling more in control, is everything tidy? Or maybe it's the other way around.

You can calm your head and find some clarity, or you can tidy the space around you to create the same feeling.

Find an area in your house - maybe a drawer or shelf - that you can tidy and de-clutter. If you're pushed for time, set a timer for ten minutes. Notice how much you get done and how satisfying it can be.

DAY SEVEN
If you need help, get help

It can be so difficult to ask for help.

Pride, fear, shame, independence - all sorts of thoughts and beliefs can stop you from reaching out.

What stops you from asking for help when you need it?

Whether it's an expert that you need, or just a cosy chat with a friend or relative, you might find that there is someone who can help you change what you're feeling or support you to success. How good does it feel when someone asks you for help? It builds relationship, connection, trust and support in both directions.

If this is difficult for you, start small and ease yourself into inviting people in.

DAY EIGHT
Meditation

The word 'meditation' can conjure up images of having to sit silently humming or chanting to yourself. It's actually a very simple technique and is incredibly powerful. The purpose of meditation is to stop your thoughts and just be in the present moment. That's much simpler than it might sound.

Try focusing on your breathing, or looking at one point - bringing all your attention into one thing.

You can meditate when you're walking, cooking, showering, creating or listening to music. Simply place all your attention on what you're doing.

Set a timer for one minute to begin with and focus on one thing, then slowly increase the time as you grow this new habit.
Notice how you feel before and after the meditation.

DAY NINE
Set your intention

How do you know when you have arrived at your destination?

If you say "I want to go on holiday", but don't decide where you want to go, how will you get there? When you know what you want, you plan and take action.

You can do this with any task or feeling that you want to create. Whatever you are doing, set an intention before you begin, to state how you want to feel or what you want to achieve.

What message do you want to communicate in a conversation?
How do you want to feel after an activity?

If your intention is to feel good, or to feel closer to someone, or to feel happier, then it's much more likely to happen when you set your goal beforehand.

DAY TEN
Finishing things - your to-do list

If you're anything like me, there's a to-do list in the back of your head of all the things you need to complete. It contains all the tasks you need to finish, as well as ideas and new projects.

Like an app open on your phone or computer, each unfinished idea is using some of your energy all the time.

If you get those ideas and tasks out of your head and onto paper, you can see what you need to do, you can plan, prioritise and start ticking them off.

Satisfying for your conscious and unconscious mind, this frees up more energy.

Give it a go; you might find you're further down your list than you thought!

DAY ELEVEN
Connect with someone

It was Mother's Day on 11th March 2021 when I created today's tip, so Happy Mother's Day to my Mum and my Step-Mum!
And to all the mothers in the world.

Whatever your relationship is with your mother, whether she is with you or not, whether it's healthy or not, you can tune in with Mother Energy and send love and connection to where it's needed. You could write to your own mother, to an ideal mother, to your inner mother, or to your child, or to your inner child. Connect with someone with loving maternal energy.

Who needs to hear from you today?

Who could you send love to and how does that feel for you?

DAY TWELVE
Tap in the positive

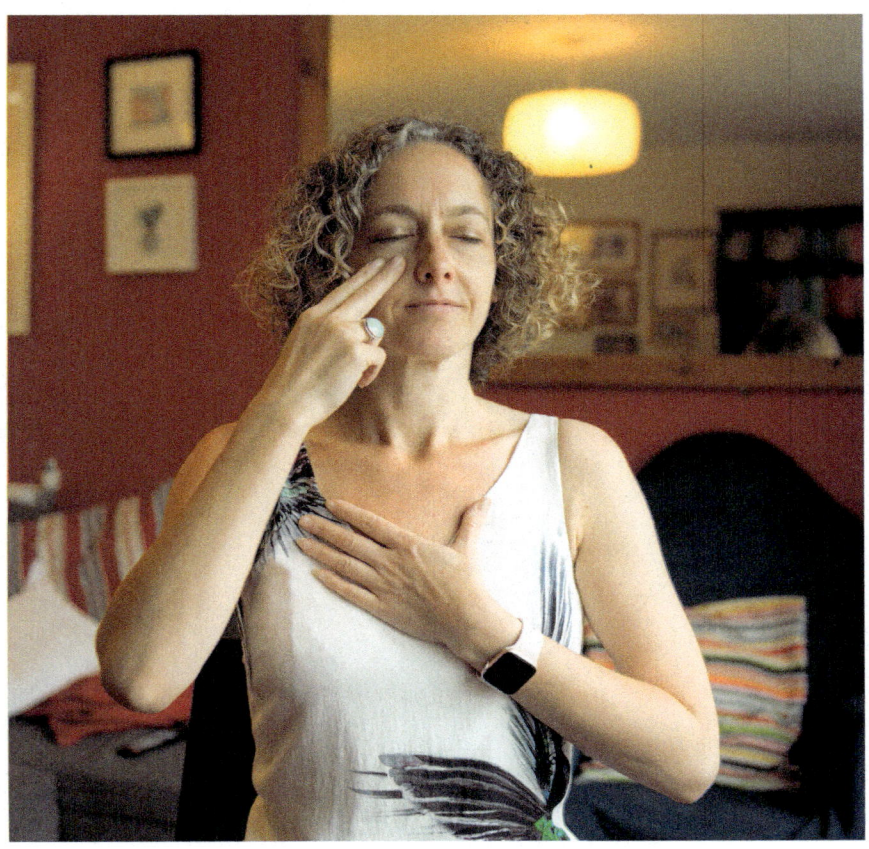

Today you're going to use EFT in a slightly different way by tapping in the positive. Choose any emotion that you want to feel e.g. peace, confidence, calm.

Start by holding one hand over your heart, take two fingers from the other hand and start tapping on top of the head, breathe and repeat:

"More …… (insert desired emotion)."
Tap through all the points repeating the phrase and feel the emotion as it builds in your body.

You can tap in as many emotions as you want.
Keep it simple and keep tapping and notice how you feel.

See Day Two for a map of the points.

DAY THIRTEEN
Tune!

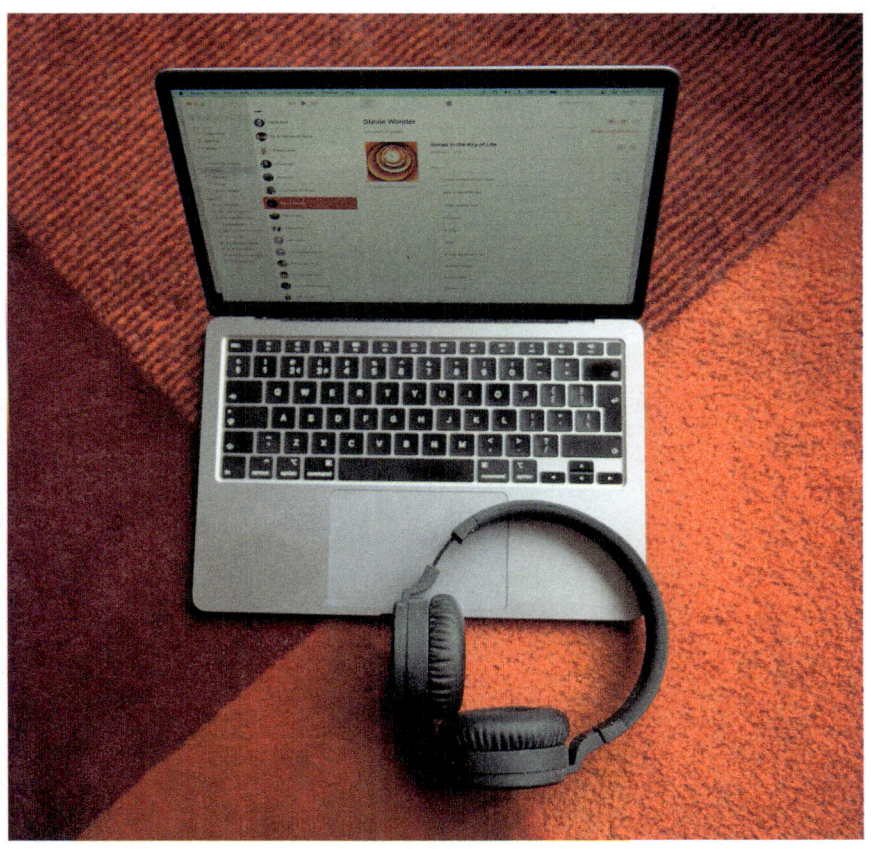

What song or piece of music helps to bring in a different state for you?

Music can shift you so quickly into a better mood and even better if it makes you want to move and dance!

What is your favourite disco floor-filler tune?

The more you listen to it and consciously choose the feeling you want to create, the quicker it will come and the better you will feel.

Why not make yourself a playlist for different emotional states?

DAY FOURTEEN
Take a different view

Today's tip is to change your perspective.

If you're too close to a situation, you might feel the emotion too intensely; you might not be able to understand what's going on.

When you zoom out and look at things from a different perspective, you might see alternative solutions or ideas that you could try.

Being above and looking down on a situation will help you to see other people's viewpoints and needs.

Step back, be objective and ask what's needed.

DAY FIFTEEN
Try hypnotherapy

Dating back to Ancient Egypt, hypnotherapy is an incredibly powerful tool for creating lasting change and improving any aspect of your life. It works by deeply relaxing the body and mind, allowing direct communication with your unconscious mind.

There are many myths surrounding hypnosis - that you are under someone else's control or that you will be programmed to do things you don't want to do. The truth is that all hypnosis is self-hypnosis. The practitioner will work with you to decide your focus. You are conscious and aware the whole time and simply creating pre-planned suggestions that the unconscious can choose to take on or not.

Your mind wants the absolute best for you and this process helps that happen.

I've recorded a session for you: stressfreelifeacademy.com/freeresources

DAY SIXTEEN
Do nothing for 5 minutes

Sit somewhere, get comfy, set a timer for five minutes and do nothing.

Just sit and be, watch the world go by and notice whatever presents itself to you.

Think what you think, feel what you feel and be in the moment.

You're probably so used to doing and achieving and getting things done, it might feel uncomfortable to stop for a few minutes - but stick with it.

You can tap away any negative emotions or allow them to float by, like weather passing through.

Take five for yourself and notice how you feel.

DAY SEVENTEEN
Get creative

Whether you want to make something, write, draw or paint, gather everything you need, and set a timer for 20 minutes; let your mind wander and express yourself in some way.

Maybe you haven't done that since you were at school?

The wonderful book *The Artist's Way* by Julia Cameron shows you how to get in touch with your creative side.

When you open up to creativity, your ideas start to flow. You are here to create something in one way or another. It doesn't have to be beautiful and you can keep it for yourself.

Find a way to express your own creativity today.

DAY EIGHTEEN
Mix it up - Do something differently

Today's tip is to increase your flexibility and adaptability. The more flexible you are, the more successful you will be. Your unconscious mind holds strategies for doing everything in your life; from making a cup of tea, driving or getting dressed, to breathing, to loving - everything.

When you consciously do things differently, you increase your flexibility as your mind will work things out again for you, always finding the most efficient way.

When life doesn't go as planned, you're able to find a way to adapt with minimum stress. You can cope with the change.

Walk around the supermarket in a different direction, drive a different route, put your socks on in a different order - these tiny little changes help to keep that open-mindedness.

DAY NINETEEN
Come up with 10 solutions to a problem

If there's something you've been trying to resolve, and you've been wondering what to do or you don't know what the next step is, use this tip:

Write down the problem at the top of the page and then write ten solutions to that problem - whatever comes to mind. You might come up with one or two ideas fairly easily but if you push through and make yourself come up with 10 ideas, your mind has to really start to think, and get more inventive.

The more you get into that zone, the more ideas can come. Even if the ideas seem silly, write them down and see what comes next.

These are nuggets of gold you're mining - dig deep!

DAY TWENTY

What's the best advice you've ever been given?

What's the best piece of advice that anyone has given you, that one phrase, or saying or moment in your life that's just clicked.

Perhaps you come back to that moment again and again and it makes you feel better.

"This too shall pass."

When things are stressful or difficult, this thought will help you relax.

Nothing stays the same forever, whatever is going on, in or around you, will one day be a memory…

Image of Bobba.

DAY TWENTY ONE

Set yourself a health challenge

It's so easy to take good health for granted and often it's only when something goes wrong that we realise how important it is. Having a health goal - or any goal - gives you a focus.

Is there a tweak you can make to you diet?
Maybe you've been meaning to start Couch to 5K, or join a dance class?

One benefit of the lockdown is that even more resources have gone online so you can take your pick. Making a commitment with someone else will make it easier - accountability is key.

Set yourself that challenge and enjoy!

DAY TWENTY TWO

Focus on what makes you happy

Wherever you focus your attention and your energy is what you will get more of. Investing yourself in the things that you love and are grateful for will not only help you feel good, it will also bring more of those into your life.

Focusing on what isn't going well is like adding your power and energy to it.

Have you ever noticed that if you talk about something, like a blue butterfly, you suddenly notice blue butterflies everywhere? This is because your unconscious mind has flagged it for you and will bring it to your attention.

Try it out - what do you want to see?

DAY TWENTY THREE
Have compassion

Life is a constant stream of stimuli and responses. Time, weather, people, actions – all these trigger emotions and behaviours from the unconscious mind, many of which we are completely unaware of on a conscious level.

You know those days when you wake up out of sorts, for no apparent reason? Everyone has days like that. If you can step back and be compassionate and responsive to people around you, you will find less conflict and fewer triggers in yourself and others.

It's also good to remember that often someone's reaction to you is nothing to do with you. It's probably an unconscious reaction from a previous experience. Don't take it personally - make it safe for people to be around you by relaxing and bringing compassion.

Who knows what positive change might happen.

DAY TWENTY FOUR
Find a rainbow

This is an easy mindfulness technique: simply look around you and find objects that are the colours of the rainbow. You can do this anywhere, at any time.

Mindfulness brings you into the present moment and finding things that are in your immediate environment is a super-fast way of doing that. Being present takes your attention away from lingering pain from the past, or any anxiety about the future.

You are right here, right now and you are safe.

Your body can't be stressed and relaxed at the same time - you are either in one state or the other. The more you can create relaxation here and now in your body, the more you can create that in other areas of your life.

DAY TWENTY FIVE
Have a bath

Not rocket science today! Having a soak is a great way to look after yourself. A salt bath with Epsom salts or Himalayan salt will relieve stress from your muscles.

Light a candle, put on some music - create a peaceful haven and use it to take care of yourself.

Relax and unwind for as long and often as you can.

Visualise the tension and worries releasing and draining away down the plughole.

What can you let go of?

DAY TWENTY SIX

Evoke the Learning State

The Learning State is brilliant if you're feeling overwhelmed by emotion or if you need to concentrate or get 'into the zone'. It's extremely simple to do and with a little practice, you will be able to shift into it quickly.

Here's what to do:
Keeping your head still, breathe in as you roll your eyes up and focus on a point on the ceiling.
Then as you slowly breathe out, drop your eyes slowly back to eye level.
Keep looking straight ahead and bring your attention to your peripheral vision.
Repeat a few times until you feel yourself settle and relax.

Check the website for a video: stressfreelifeacademy.com/freeresources

DAY TWENTY SEVEN

What's the kindest thing you could say to yourself?

You're probably aware of a critical voice that can pop up in your head.

For some, it's a constant presence; for others it comes and goes, usually appearing at the most stressful moments. What's interesting is that we will often listen to this voice and believe what it says. If a friend was talking to you like that, you would probably not want to spend time with them.

Often that voice says things that you wouldn't dream of saying to anyone else. Why does it have such power? To counteract it, what is the kindest thing you can say to yourself in response?

How can you be your own best friend?
If you were being extremely kind to yourself, what would you say?

DAY TWENTY EIGHT

What advice would you give your younger self?

As the phrase goes, 'Hindsight is a wonderful thing.' Often, you need to go through an experience to get the learning from it, which is a Catch 22 situation. I have discovered that the advice you would give a younger version of yourself is the advice you need to hear right now.

Think back to a difficult time in your past and ask yourself:

"What do I wish I had known then?"
"What would I like to remind myself of?"
"What got me through to resolution?"
"What did I learn from it?"

As always, notice what you notice and let the answers come to you.

You are wiser than you know…

DAY TWENTY NINE
Drink more water

Another simple one today, but it is often forgotten or overlooked: drink more water. Your body is made up of around 60% water.

Did you know that by the time you feel thirsty, you are already dehydrated?

This can cause stress in the body, increasing cortisol levels and affecting your energy, your mood and all the systems of your body.

Aim to drink around eight glasses of water per day.

Try it for a few days and notice how you feel.

DAY THIRTY
If you ran a shop, what would you sell?

Today's tip comes from '*The School of Life's Career Crisis Prompt Card Pack*'.

I've chosen this question:

"If I was forced to run a shop, it would sell…"

Anything that makes you think differently is going to benefit you.

What do you enjoy?
What do you love?
What's your passion?

Let your mind run with that thought, have a little daydream and see where it takes you…

DAY THIRTY ONE
Walk down a path you've never been down before

It's so easy to get stuck in to routines, to do the same things week in, week out.

It can be a struggle to make time for yourself.

Your mind creates new habits and patterns all the time.

You often won't be aware of it as the unconscious mind simply takes care of things for you so that you don't have to actively think about what you're doing.

Today look for something you've never seen before, or try looking at something familiar in a new light.

Keep on keeping it fresh.

DAY THIRTY TWO

List your 10 best qualities

fun

energetic *expressive*

caring *relaxed*

reliable *loving*

awesome *affectionate*

compassionate

What are your best bits?

Find your ten best qualities.

How would your friends describe you?
What do like about yourself?

It can be so easy to get into a negative spiral of thoughts when things go wrong. Self-criticism and that negative inner voice can hurt.

Find ten good things about yourself that you do well and refer back to it whenever you need a boost.

DAY THIRTY THREE

Focus on your future self

If you've ever had a 1:1 session with me, you will know that I often end with a 'future self' image. This is where you see yourself in the future, having resolved the issue you are going through at present. You can connect with the future you, ask advice, borrow feelings of confidence, ease, satisfaction, whatever it is that you want to feel right now.

The more you can visualise and feel the resolution, the quicker it will manifest. Close your eyes, see yourself in the future and 'step in' to the picture. Connect with your future self. Invite the future you to step into your body now so you can experience what it feels like to be at that point.

'Download' this feeling and remember it. You can access it whenever you need to. This is incredibly powerful and gives you great insight.

DAY THIRTY FOUR

Take one tiny step towards your goal

Following on from yesterday's tip of visiting your future self and getting an idea of what's coming your way, you can go even further.

Re-create the future self feeling again - see what you saw, hear what you heard and feel what you felt.

Now ask yourself:
"What is my next step towards this goal?"
"What one tiny thing can I do today to get me there? "

Trust what comes up and take action.

If the step feels overwhelming, break it down to smaller chunks until it feels ridiculously easy and manageable. Use that momentum, keep going and don't stop until you've got to where you want to be.

DAY THIRTY FIVE
List all the good things and good people in your life

Take some time, grab a pen and paper and list all the good things that have happened to you. Let all the good people and experiences, the places you love and what you have loved doing bubble to the surface.

Appreciating all that good stuff will feel amazing. Do your best to acknowledge just how far you've come and how loved you are. If you struggle with this, then think about what you would like to create in the future.

Where would you like to go?
What's missing in your life?

Now's the time to create the life you want.

DAY THIRTY SIX
Describe a happy memory

Yesterday's tip was about finding people, places, situations and memories that you value and appreciate and bringing them to mind. Today's step is to choose one of those memories and make it as real as you can.

Describe it in words, or even draw a picture or diagram. Find something that inspires the feeling of it. Feel what you felt, hear what you heard, see what you saw and really get into the energy of that moment or what it was like to be there.

The more you 'supercharge' that feeling, the more of those experiences will come into your life. If you make one of those past moments real in your mind and body and truly value and enjoy it, you'll get more of those feelings.

Bliss!

DAY THIRTY SEVEN

Stop pushing - What self-care do you need?

When I was recording the video for this day's tip - originally about negative emotions - I did about 25 takes; my camera kept playing up, I got too hot, it got too noisy. All these little things were getting in the way so I stopped, went home, had a cup of tea and took a break.

I needed to stop pushing.

Do you ever get those moments when it just feels like a "NO" at every turn? Sometimes it's right to push through, and other days it's best to stop and try again later

What self-care can you give yourself today?
What can you say 'No' to?

DAY THIRTY EIGHT
Emergency tapping

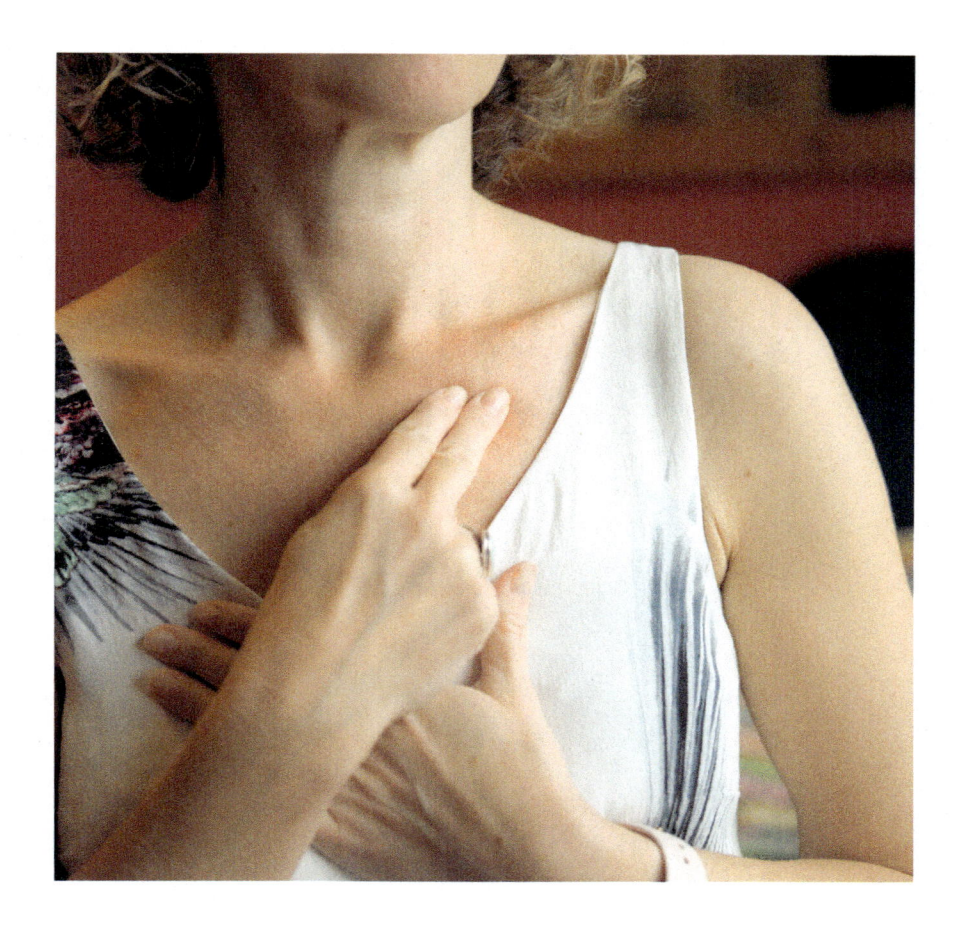

The collarbone tapping point is what I call the 'Emergency Tapping Point.'

This point is on the kidney meridian and, among other things, relates to feelings of fear, guilt, nervousness, lack of confidence and wanting to run from situations rather than face them.

When you're stressed out, having a difficult conversation, feeling anxious or upset, simply tap on this point and breathe.

Gently tap, rub or hold these points until your body starts to feel calmer and more relaxed.

DAY THIRTY NINE
Get organised

Getting organised and recognising what you want to get done on a monthly, weekly or daily basis can have a huge impact on your stress levels.

Do you ever wish someone would take over and tell you what to do?

If you decide what you want to achieve in a day the night before, all that's left is for you to get up and do. It's like someone else left you instructions to follow and you just tick them off.

Starting your day or work session with 3 clear objectives in mind will save you valuable time and head space. Life happens and plans can change, but getting organised will keep you on track towards achieving your goals.

DAY FORTY
Make a decision

Today's tip might seem straightforward - but it's not always easy to do.

If you've been hesitating about an issue, it can feel daunting to make a decision. Turning it over in your mind takes energy; you may worry about what others might think, or you may be scared of getting it wrong. Making a decision will bring relief and take the pressure off.

Action (even the 'wrong' action), beats inaction every time.

Keep moving and fine-tuning your next step, you will get where you need to be.

What decision do you need to make today?

DAY FORTY ONE
Your body language

Your mind and body are connected and inform each other continually.

If you're feeling sad, your shoulders might hunch over and you shrink into yourself. If you're feeling good, your posture will be more open, your head lifted high and eyes alert.

Notice what you're feeling and what your body is telling you.

Are they in agreement?

Change your posture to reflect the state that you want to feel.

The Super Hero pose is a good one for confidence (as my five-year-old self is demonstrating for you here. Wonder Woman was my hero!)

DAY FORTY TWO
Watch your language

Have you ever noticed how you speak to yourself?

How do you describe yourself to people?
Whatever you say, your mind will believe.

You might say things like: "I'm always late," or "I never remember people's names," or "I can't do maths".

Ask the people around you what they have noticed about your language. It reveals what's going on under the surface, in your unconscious mind. When you bring awareness to how it is at this moment, you can consciously choose new beliefs about yourself.

What do you want to believe?

DAY FORTY THREE

Say "no" if it's a "no"

Boundaries are a key element to your stress-free life.

Being willing to put your needs in front of others' and doing what's right for you can be hard, but it helps everyone in the long run.

Essentially, it is saying "no" to the things you don't want and "yes" to the things you do want.

Were you relieved when lockdown started and gave you an excuse to say "no"?

If you find it hard to keep the boundary, first be honest with yourself and decide what you do and don't want. Start practising saying "yes" or "no" to different things and strengthen your inner boundary.

DAY FORTY FOUR
Tense and release

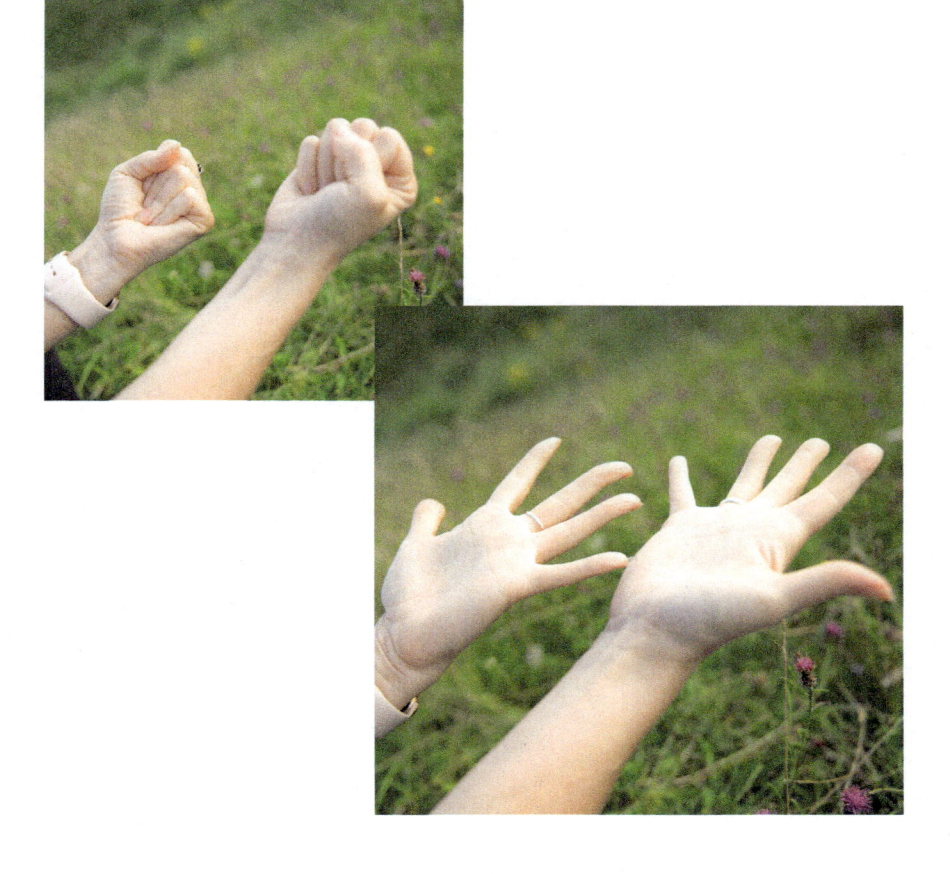

This is a great way to release stress and tension from your body. It is particularly good if you can't get to sleep or if your mind is racing.

Find a comfortable position, either lying down or sitting, and take a few easy deep breaths.

Now breathe in, hold it and tense every muscle in your body. Squeeze everything as tight as you can… then breathe out and let it all go.

Repeat this twice, holding every muscle tight each time, and feeling the release as you let go. Notice how you feel, how your muscles feel, how that tension eases, releases and relaxes.

DAY FORTY FIVE
Write down your worries and three things you are grateful for

Reflecting on your day and writing down any thoughts before you go to sleep is a great way to process the stress of the day.

Getting tasks out of your head and on to the page is an action step and you can mentally tick it off your list for the night.

Recognising at least three things that have gone well throughout the day, moments that you appreciate, however small, will shift the balance into the positive again.

Appreciation is a powerful emotion for releasing stress from the body.

DAY FORTY SIX
Good sleep routine

Do you have a healthy bedtime routine?
Bad sleep can dramatically impact your stress levels.

Do you fall asleep quickly but then wake up?
Do you toss and turn for hours and then wake up feeling groggy?

Be observant and notice what's working or not working for you.
What changes can you make in order to get the sleep that you need?

Small tweaks to your habits can have a big impact. Try going to bed earlier, having a night-time tea, reading before sleep or getting up at the same time every morning. Check in with yourself, trust your intuition and try out some changes to see what helps you.

DAY FORTY SEVEN
It's OK not to be OK

There are days when you just don't feel OK.

You try everything, but you just can't feel good.

Your energy is low, you feel flat and you don't know why.

Take the pressure off and remember it is OK not to be OK, and it is OK to be where you are. The term 'duvet day' sums it up. Sometimes you just need a day off.

On those low days, do your best, do the minimum you can and know that it will all be different again soon.

Go with it and be in the present moment.

DAY FORTY EIGHT

Procrastination

Resistance, procrastination and self-sabotage. These are the types of behaviour you do to stop yourself from achieving your goals. But why?!

Usually it's because of a hidden fear, or underlying limiting belief in your unconscious mind.

What's your favourite way to procrastinate?
Do you always have to tidy up or feel you need more time/energy/money in place before you start on something for you?

As always, awareness is the first step to change. Notice the feeling, feel the fear, knuckle down and do what you have to do.

DAY FORTY NINE
Overcome overwhelm

Overwhelm can create procrastination and stop you in your tracks.

A great NLP technique to use to break through overwhelm is 'chunking down.'

Make a big job smaller, into easier and more manageable steps - the tinier the better - to get started.

If you want to run a marathon, you don't just go out and run a race without preparation. The first thing you need is a pair of shoes and the step before that is to decide where you will get them.

Maybe you first need to chat to a friend who runs for advice.

Keep working back until the next step feels easy and take it from there.

DAY FIFTY
Keep going

It's day 50! You're halfway through!

It's so important to celebrate your successes along the way.

Your unconscious mind can be like training a puppy - it needs lots of positive reinforcement and rewards to keep it on track.

Remember to ask for help if you need it and don't stop until you get where you are going.

You don't know what's around the corner - enjoy every day that you can.

DAY FIFTY ONE

Choose a word for the day - Peace

peace

laurapridencecalligraphy.co.uk

Today choose a word that encompasses how you want to feel.

It could be anything: peaceful, relaxed, calm, successful, happy, confident, successful, free, loving, abundant, compassionate, joyful, focussed…

When you have chosen your word, feel it in your body.

Think of things that grow the feeling.

Throughout your day, keep coming back to the word and the feeling it invokes.

DAY FIFTY TWO
Look around you with fresh eyes

Your unconscious mind will delete, distort and generalise all the information coming in through your senses. It does this to help you as there is only so much you can focus on consciously.

You have a relationship with everything around you so it's important to surround yourself with things which lift you.

Today, walk around one room or your home with fresh eyes. Look at each item and notice how it makes you feel.

Take your time and make any changes that you need to.
What do you need to remove or bring in?

DAY FIFTY THREE
Have a nap

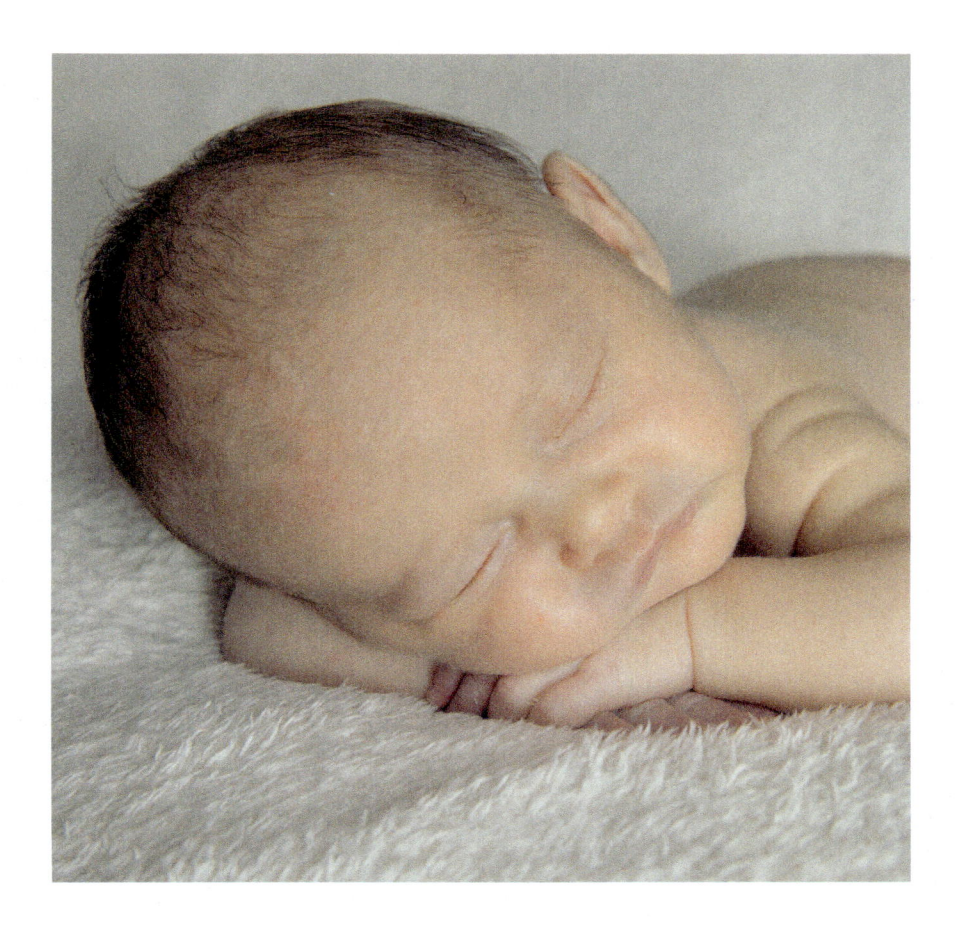

The best way to reduce your stress is to stop your thoughts.

The problem is often not what you're going through, but how you feel about it.

Having a nap for 10 minutes at any point in your day will help you in many ways: it will recharge your energy, boost your mood, improve your night-time sleep and give your mind and body a rest.

The aim is to relax and let go of any negative thoughts.

Give it a go if you've got the time. Set a timer and notice how different you feel on the days that you take time to rest.

DAY FIFTY FOUR
Hot & Cold emotions game

Did you ever play this game when you were young?

Someone hid an object that you had to find and they would say 'hotter' or 'colder' as you got closer to or further away from it? (It's good fun, give it a go!)

Your emotions work in the same way. The way you feel tells you whether you are getting closer to or further away from what you want. The thoughts making you feel good are moving you in the right direction. The ones that feel uncomfortable are taking you away from what you want, so let those go and return to a thought which brings relief.

You have an emotional response to whatever you're focusing on. Choose subjects that lift your mood and that you enjoy thinking about as much as you can.

DAY FIFTY FIVE
Let the Earth support you

Today, connect with the Earth.

Lie down or have your bare feet on the ground and breathe; let the Earth support you.

It's so easy to get caught up in the worries and stresses of the day.

Tune into the hugeness of the planet and your problems might seem a little smaller and more manageable.

Let go and be supported. It feels amazing!

DAY FIFTY SIX
Respond rather than react

The Second Arrow is a Buddhist concept and teaches about your responses.

The first arrow is an external 'attack' - an argument, or something happening to you. The second arrow is your reaction to that event.

You get to choose your response and if it hurts you or not.

Do you bite back or take a breath and choose before reacting in a conversation?

Do you tell everyone when something bad happens (more arrows) or do you learn from it, turn it around and choose something that feels good..

DAY FIFTY SEVEN
Havening

Today I want to share a technique called 'havening', or creating a haven for yourself. It helps to relax your body and calm the stress response.

Think of comforting a child or an animal with gentle reassurance.

It's a natural response.

Bring your hands to the tops of your opposite shoulders and gently stroke down the sides of your upper arms, breathing easily.

Keep going until you feel yourself relax and let go.

DAY FIFTY EIGHT
Happy buttons

Holding your 'happy buttons' will help to reduce the stress response in your body. It is a great thing to use for yourself, or for young children.

When the body is in stress, the blood rushes to the reptilian part of the brain at the back of the head. You want to draw the energy back to the front of the head, where the thinking happens. It helps calm the system and allows you to think clearly again.

Take three fingers and press them gently against your forehead above your eyes.
You may feel a pulse there.
Breathe.
Hold it for a few seconds and feel the change in your focus.

DAY FIFTY NINE
Heartmath Breathing Technique

Heartmath Breathing™ is another quick and easy way to come out of the stress response and into rest and relaxation. It was originally created to help people get into a more productive and effective state of mind.

Close your eyes, relax, place your hands over your heart.

Bring to mind a person or a place, that feels good and creates a feeling of gratitude and appreciation.

Breathe in and out effortlessly and easily to a count of 5 or 6, without pausing between the in and out breath.

Continue this for 5 or 6 breaths or until you feel the shift in your body.

Visit www.heartmath.org for more information.

DAY SIXTY
Trust the process

When you set your intention for something and start moving towards it, you need to accept what happens and allow events to unfold. It might not be what you expect.

You don't plant seeds and then dig them up to see if they've sprouted.

You don't put a cake in the oven and keep opening the door to see if it's ready.

Set your intention, take action and then let it happen.

The more you can trust in the process, trust that you're getting it right and trust in yourself, the easier it will be.

DAY SIXTY ONE
Give yourself a break

Do you have a nagging, unhelpful habit that you're constantly drawn to but wish you didn't do, such as doubting yourself, or spending too much time on social media?

Maybe you're always half-finishing things, or putting everyone else first?

Give yourself a break; hit pause, draw a line in the sand and decide - just for today - that you're not going to do it anymore. If you catch yourself slipping back into the 'bad' habit, re-align, re-commit and keep going.

Clear boundaries bring endless freedom.

DAY SIXTY TWO
Forgive something from your past

Your unconscious mind remembers everything you've ever experienced.
It's like a computer that runs programmes on repeat.

Some of those programmes, or beliefs and patterns of behaviour, need updating in order for you to feel more relaxed, peaceful and calmer. Let go and forgive yourself for those difficult moments from the past.

You might need to work with a professional to clear the deeper, trickier memories but it can be very helpful to write a therapeutic letter (one that you never send) to a younger you, or someone from your past to resolve an old pain.

You can't change the past but you can change how you feel about it.

It's never too late to make amends.

DAY SIXTY THREE

List ten things that went well

Part of your mind is always on the look out for the things that could go wrong. It's a common mind trap that anyone can fall in to - only noticing the negative. Remembering events that went well and felt good will help to counteract this habit.

List ten things that worked out well for you, that were better than expected, things that were a success. It doesn't have to be big. Lots of tiny, everyday moments are often more powerful than one big shiny moment - although those are great too.

Add to the list as you keep noticing how successful you really are.

DAY SIXTY FOUR
Eat an apple mindfully

Being present and living in the moment is all there truly is.

When your attention is not in the past and not in the future and you're right here, right now you are more relaxed and focusing on what's real.

When you use all of your senses: sight, sound, sensation, taste and smell, you are fully engaged in where you are.

To experience this, take your time to eat an apple, close your eyes, hear the crunch taste it, enjoy it, feel the goodness going into your body.

Have a moment with your apple and enjoy!

DAY SIXTY FIVE
See how far you've come

Take stock, look and recognise the journey that you have been on.

You are not the same person you were a year ago, five years ago or ten years ago.

When you feel like you're treading water day to day, that you don't have time for yourself and are constantly stressed out, you forget that you are making progress.

Acknowledge what you have achieved, how much you have grown and be proud.

You are amazing!

DAY SIXTY SIX
Comfort break

Make time today to attend to your self care.

Everyone has needs and expectations. Often these are placed on other people. When you meet your own needs and look after yourself with deep care, you pave the way for others to do the same.

How do you like to comfort yourself?
Maybe snuggling under a blanket with a book and a cuppa?
Maybe watching a movie with someone you love?

What can you do to give yourself some basic comfort?

Give yourself permission to relax and simply be.

DAY SIXTY SEVEN
Morning Pages

Today's tip comes from the book '*The Artist's Way*' by Julia Cameron. It's a wonderful book designed to re-connect you to or strengthen your creativity.

The Morning Pages is a simple but powerful exercise. On rising in the morning, sit and write three pages without stopping - a stream of consciousness. You don't need to have an aim, a purpose or even a subject matter. Let the words flow.

This clears your mind and gets the extraneous thoughts and wonderings out of the way. Underneath these thoughts, you get to the ideas, inspirations, and solutions - the rich layers of your creativity beneath the mindless chatter.

Try it every day for a week or a month and notice how you feel.

You will be so glad you did.

DAY SIXTY EIGHT
Loving Kindness Meditation

Here is a Buddhist practice called '*Loving Kindness Meditation*'. It is a simple, gentle and lovely way to connect with yourself and with others.
Get comfortable, relax and place your hands over your heart or in your lap.
Close your eyes and repeat the phrase:

"May you be well. May you be happy.
May you be filled with Loving Kindness".

First direct these words to yourself.
Then direct them to someone that you love.
Then direct them to someone you are in conflict with.

You can repeat this every day as many times as you need to.
If you have a difficult relationship with someone, keep focusing on them and see what magic happens to heal between you.

DAY SIXTY NINE
White Light Meditation

Meditation doesn't have to be sitting motionless in silence but the purpose of it is to calm your thoughts and to stop the 'monkey mind'. This is another easy method to try.

Get comfortable, either sitting or lying down and close your eyes. Take a few breaths and imagine white light coming in through your head, down through your spine and spreading into your body, into your heart, down your arms to your fingers, down your legs to your toes.

If you notice any tension or aches and pains, place your hand over that area and focus white light into it. Feel it soothing every cell and organ in your body.

With every breath in notice any tension or stress and with every breath out, let it go. You can do this as often and for as long as you want to.

DAY SEVENTY
Silence

The world is a noisy place. There is a constant bombardment of information, deadlines, pressure, world events - the stress triggers can be everywhere if you let them.

Silence can be a rare thing. When it is silent, you might notice sensations and feelings bubbling up. Often what you want to avoid comes up in these moments, which is natural and nothing to worry about. Listen to what arises and breathe to let it go.

Have you ever noticed some people feel the need to fill the space in a lull in conversation. Maybe they are feeling uncomfortable and exposed when the noise has subsided...

Let the silence happen and let it speak to you.

DAY SEVENTY ONE

Write with your non-dominant hand

Today you are going to tune into your inner wisdom.

You will need pen, paper and time and space for yourself.

What issue or problem do you want to resolve?
Write this at the top of the page.
Ask a question by writing it with your dominant hand.
Switch the pen to your non-dominant hand and simply write the response.

This exercise can give you a great insight into what's going on under the surface of your mind and bring a fresh perspective.
It can be revealing, interesting and fun.

Your unconscious mind has the answer, let it speak to you.

DAY SEVENTY TWO

Move into the learning zone

brightfeather.studio

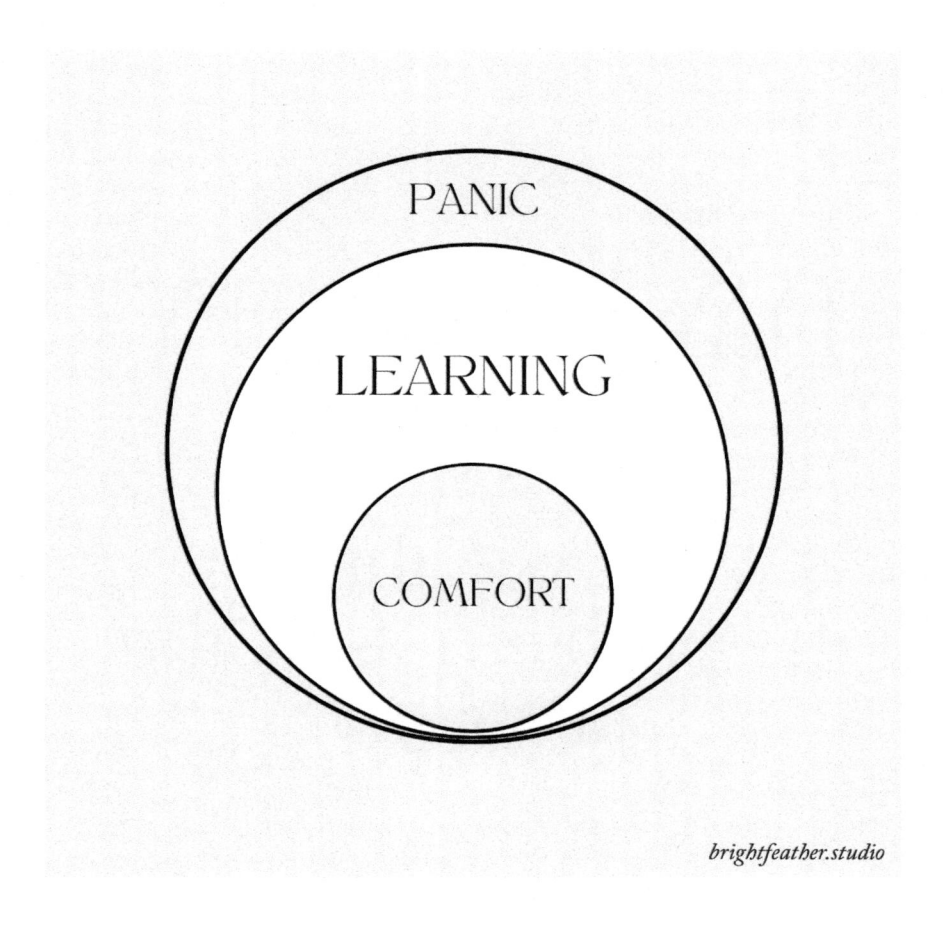

Change can be challenging and too much too soon can put you off forever. Life is forever expanding, however, and if you're not learning and growing then you could be stagnating.

When you are in your Comfort Zone, you feel safe and in control - you know what you're doing.

When you learn something new, you can either move into the Learning Zone - ease your way in with support, getting used to the new way or dive straight into the deep end - the Panic Zone!

You will know your own style. As long as you're always pushing the boundaries in one way or another, you will stay fresh and adaptable.

DAY SEVENTY THREE

What you think is the problem, isn't the problem

Often the things you're dealing with day-to-day are not really the problem: they are symptoms of the problem. The real issue is likely to be an underlying belief about yourself, such as "I'm not good enough."

Your beliefs filter the way you see the world. Each experience is assessed through this filter and triggers a feeling, which in turn triggers a behaviour. You can work through your emotions and behaviours one at a time, or you can change your beliefs and make a positive impact on hundreds of behaviours. Beliefs are decisions made due to past experiences and are largely created in the first six years of life, when you first experience emotions.

The next time you feel uncomfortable, ask yourself: "What is the problem?" Notice the answer, and then ask yourself: "What is the problem really?". Keep asking yourself until you get to the heart of what's driving the emotions.

DAY SEVENTY FOUR
Clear out your old clothes

The clothes you wear are a direct expression of yourself and communicate to the world. Different items can impact your mood and your posture.

Think about the last time you went to an important meeting or a large social gathering. First impressions are so important and you probably spent some time deciding what to wear.

Getting rid of old clothes that don't suit you anymore or don't feel right is a great way of building self-confidence. Making conscious decisions helps you feel more in control.

What outfit expresses who you are today?

DAY SEVENTY FIVE
What would... do

Wouldn't it be lovely if someone else could step in and take over your responsibilities for a while?

Who do you admire or respect who would know just what you need?

For them it would be easy, they would know exactly what to do.
Borrow their energy for a moment.
How would they respond?
What advice would they give?

Use your imagination to open up the possibilities of another person's viewpoint and how they might see a stressful situation.

DAY SEVENTY SIX
Act as if

Take a step further from yesterday's tip, which was to look at your own situation from another person's viewpoint - now imagine actually being them for a moment.

Adopt their body language and embody their energy.

What does it feel like to have their confidence and perspective of the world?

Like taking on a role in a play, try it out and notice how it feels.

'Fake it til you make it' can help you get through those moments when you just need a little help from a friend..

DAY SEVENTY SEVEN
4-7-8 Breathing Technique

HOLD

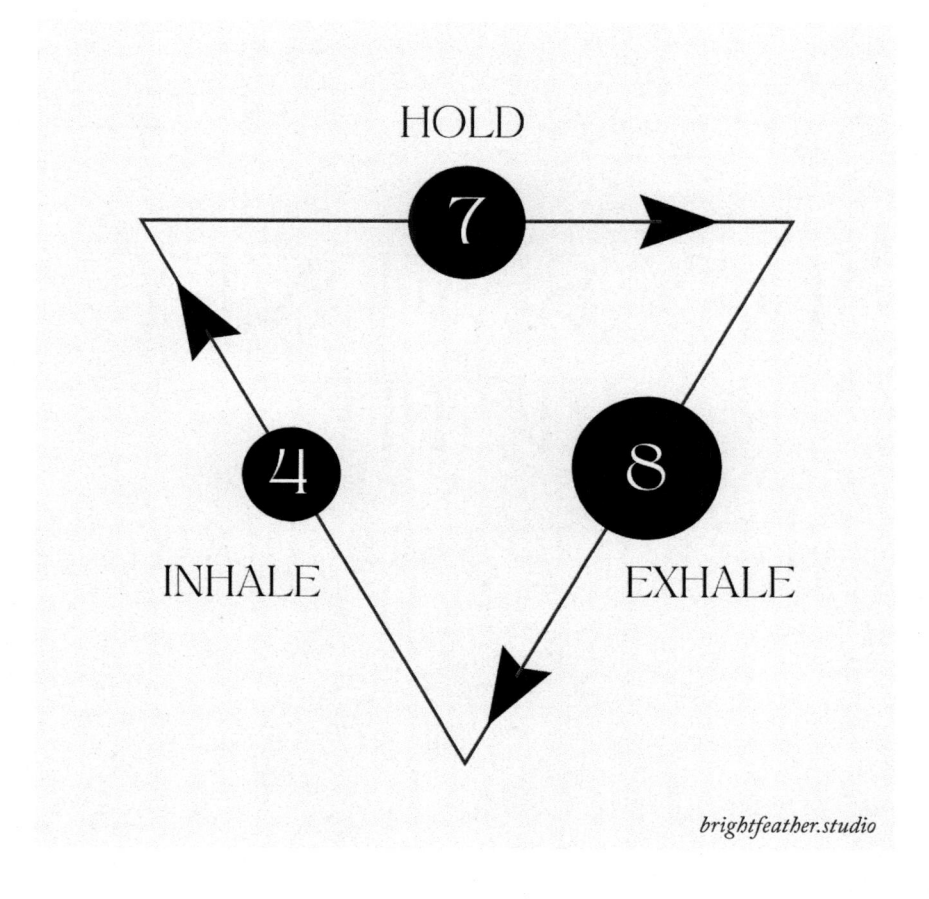

INHALE

EXHALE

brightfeather.studio

There are many breathing techniques and they all aim to return your body to a relaxed, calm state.

'4-7-8 Breathing' is a technique that you can use anywhere, at any time. You may feel a little light-headed initially, so make sure you're sitting down when you first try it.

Hold your tongue behind your top front teeth.
Breathe in for a count of 4.
Hold for a count of 7.
Breathe out for a count of 8.

Repeat 3 or 4 times and feel the shift as your whole body becomes calmer.

DAY SEVENTY EIGHT
Listen to your body

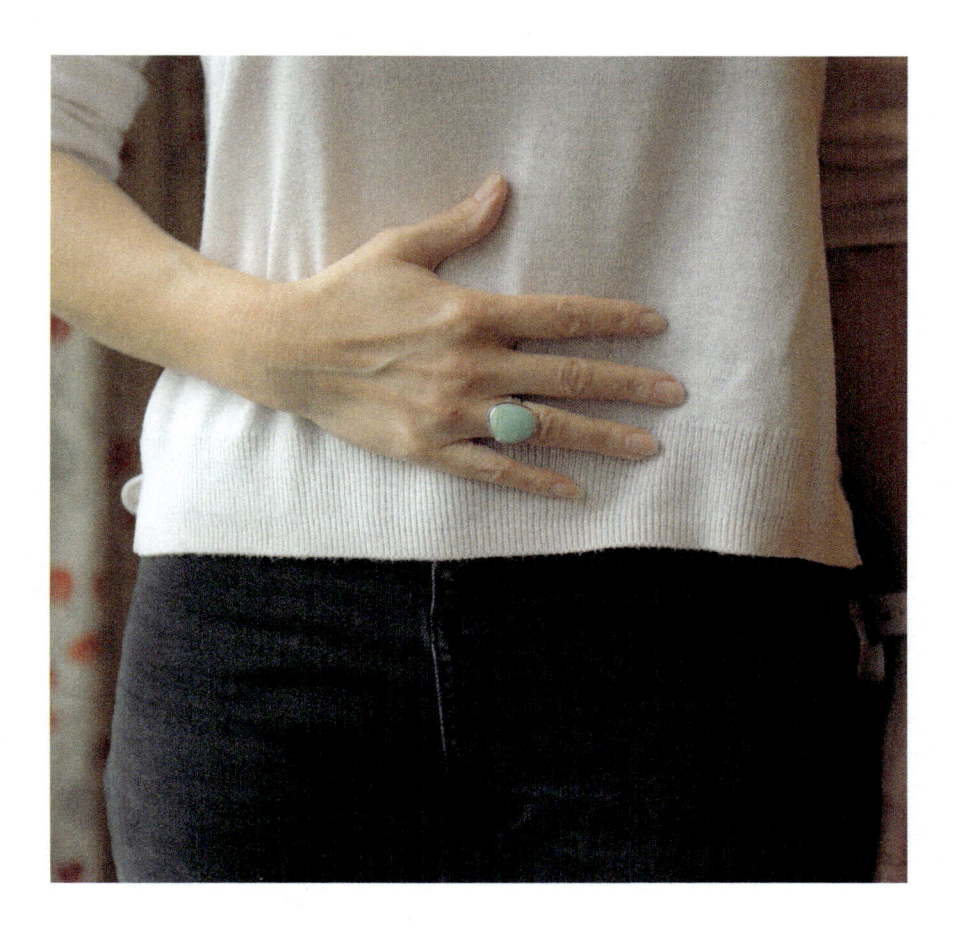

When you were little, were you made to eat everything on your plate before you were allowed dessert? While this made sure you got your 5-a-day, it impacted the conversation between you and your body. You had to override the feeling of being full in order to have a treat. The communication with your body is still there and, like any relationship, it needs to be listened to and nurtured. Take time to pay attention to the signs and signals.

You might call it intuition, insight or gut instinct, but deep down, part of you knows what you need. Connect with your body, breathe and ask it a question: "What do I need?", "What should I do about…?", or "How do I feel about this?", and listen for an answer.

The more you do this, the stronger your internal relationship becomes. You're building trust in yourself, your intuition, self-belief, self-confidence and being your own best friend. Enjoy!

DAY SEVENTY NINE
Count something

Everything in this book is designed to help you move out of stress and into rest and relaxation, or from Sympathetic (aka Fight/Flight/Freeze) to Parasympathetic Nervous Systems, to give them their official names.

The Sympathetic state means you are on high alert for danger.
Your energy is focused on survival.
When you are in the Parasympathetic state, your body is working well and is relaxed.

Look around you, acknowledge you are safe here and now.

Counting objects is a quick way of doing this. You can count window panes or floorboards, stripes on a sweater or clouds in the sky - whatever you can see around you. You might notice a sigh, a yawn or a tummy rumble - all good signs that you are back to a relaxed state.

DAY EIGHTY
Who needs your help?

You will be aware of the phrase 'there's always someone worse off than you'.

It's true - you don't have to go far to find suffering in the world. This can be stressful in itself.

Ask yourself: "Who needs my help?" A name or a person will come to mind.

Put your attention on them for a few moments. In your mind's eye, picture them receiving help, doing well and successfully overcoming whatever they are going through, easily and effortlessly.

You don't know what impact that will have on them, but it will certainly help you, and when you help yourself and bring others along with you, the whole world benefits.

Spread your love wherever it's needed today.

DAY EIGHTY ONE
Exercise

Today's tip is to exercise: move your body, get out there and raise your heart rate to increase circulation. The lymph system, which keeps you healthy as part of the immune system, needs the movement of your muscles to work efficiently.

When your body is stressed, hormones such as cortisol and adrenalin flood your system, making you feel wired, foggy and restless.

Exercise helps to clear these hormones and calm your body again. It also releases endorphins which naturally boost your mood. It's amazing what even a short walk can do to lower anxiety and stress.

DAY EIGHTY TWO
'Eat the frog'

Do you know the phrase 'eat the frog?'

The 'frog' is a task that you don't want to do and are avoiding at all costs! Your job in these moments is to find a way to make that task palatable so that you can get it done.

Make it fun, ask for help if you need to, break it down into smaller and more manageable chunks, get rewards lined up - whatever you can do to complete a task you've been dreading.

Who would you ask to help you eat the frog?

Once you're successful, make sure you celebrate and feel proud of what you have achieved!

DAY EIGHTY THREE
Go fast go alone, go far go together

The African proverb 'If you want to go fast, go alone; if you want to go far, go together' is a great message of community and a reminder of how we all need each other, in one way or another.

Independence is so important, but denying any help and support that is available to you can become a negative habit.

Do you feel you are struggling alone with something?
Do you catch yourself complaining that you have to do everything yourself?

There can be hidden beliefs that it's not OK to ask for help, or that success has to be hard fought.

Take it easy on yourself, get an expert in and notice how your stress starts to release when you find a solution. Let go and let the help in.

DAY EIGHTY FOUR
Projection

Projection is when you judge someone's behavior, making assumptions about what they are believing, thinking or feeling.

Maybe you saw a friend in the street and they blanked you. Your mind will react in any number of ways to that: they ignored me, they don't like me, it's because I didn't return their call last week, and so on.

The truth is probably that the sun was in their eyes, or their attention was elsewhere and they simply didn't see you.

Check in with what your mind is telling you, and then check the facts, what you know to be true. You might be surprised at the judgements you unconsciously make at times.

DAY EIGHTY FIVE
Tap to ground yourself

When you're grounded, you feel calm, relaxed and more present, as if you are fully in your body.

Stress can leave you feeling light-headed or disconnected from reality.

Tap repeatedly on the top of the head and then on the collarbone - around 7 times on each point - and feel the energy coming down through your body, into your feet, into your toes, down into the ground.

Repeat this until your breathing settles and you feel more relaxed.

You can repeat the phrase, "More grounded" as you tap and breathe.

DAY EIGHTY SIX
Laugh!

Humour and laughter can shift your mood and lighten a situation so quickly. Just like hearing an uplifting song, laughing can change your emotional state instantly.

Laughter is good for you in many ways: it activates and then relieves the stress response, releasing pent-up tension.

Studies have shown how often children laugh (around 300 times per day on average) compared to adults (around 20).

The sound alone of children giggling can bring a smile to your face.

Spread some laughs and share your favourite joke with someone today.

DAY EIGHTY SEVEN
Change your thoughts

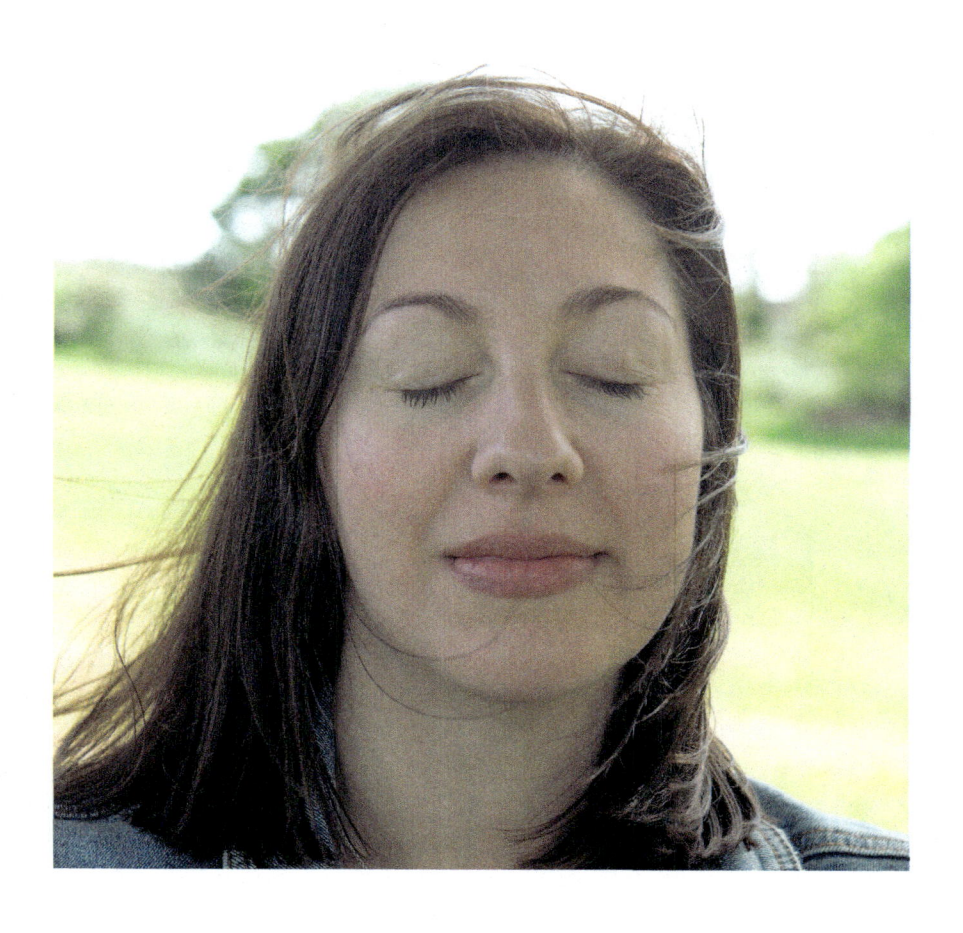

You have literally thousands of thoughts per day.
Some of these trigger reactions in your body and mind that can send you spiralling into worst-case scenarios.

When you're going through a difficult situation, thoughts about what might go wrong are often a bigger cause of stress than the actual event. When you start to catch your thoughts, question their validity and instead choose to think more positively, you can really turn things around. For example:

"I shouldn't be late" could become "I will get there at the right time"'
"I'm not getting this right" could turn into: "Maybe I'm learning something new from this"

Reach for the thoughts that feel best for you and bring relief, and you're on the right track.

DAY EIGHTY EIGHT

Plan a surprise for someone

Have you ever found a forgotten fiver in your jacket pocket?
It feels like such a bonus!

Imagine passing that feeling on to someone else out in the world.

You could pay for an extra coffee next time you buy yourself one, or hide a five-pound note in a library book; knowing that someone will receive that little surprise can lift you out of yourself.

Who knows what ripple effect your anonymous gift may cause!

Pay it forward today.

DAY EIGHTY NINE
Don't put it off

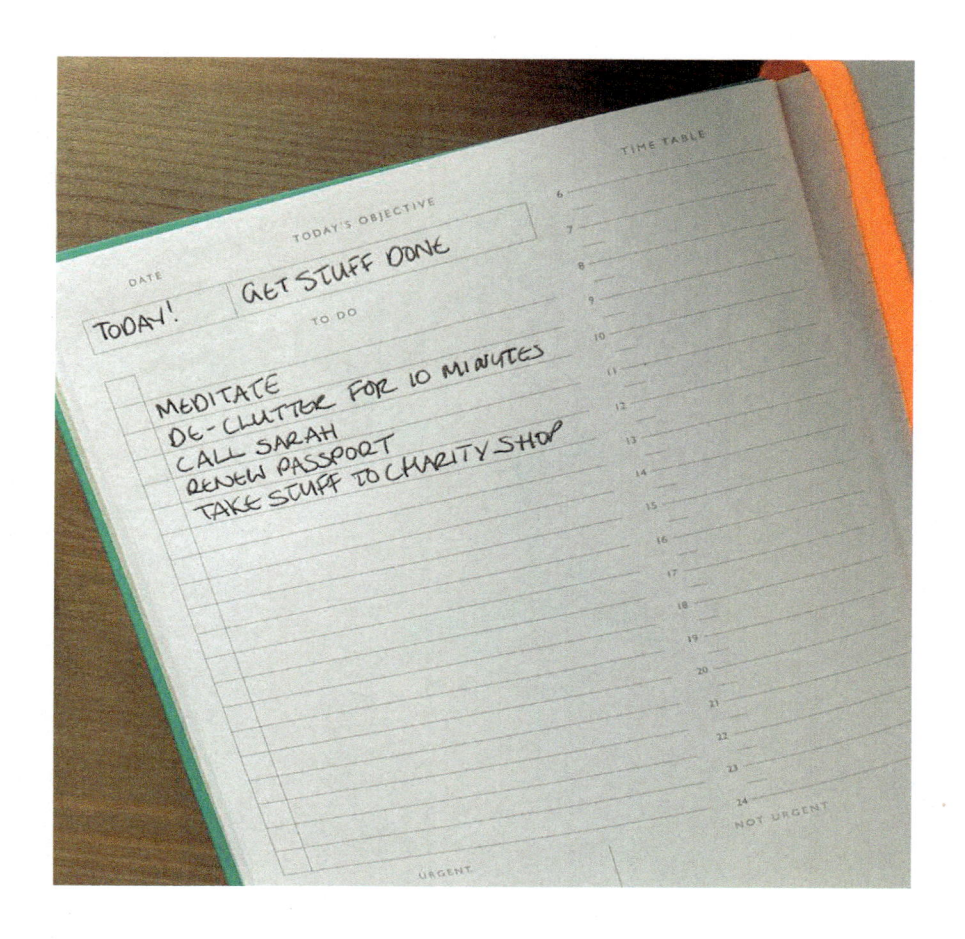

How often have you put off a job for ages, to then finally get it done in ten minutes?!

Are there things that you're putting off because you feel you haven't got what you need? Taking action will bring you the success you are striving for.

Think for a moment about the task that you push to one side because other things take priority.

Get it done, tick it off the list and feel super-proud of yourself!

Sometimes procrastination gives you a reason to be hard on yourself: don't let it. Grab the day with both hands, do what you need to do and let the good feelings in.

DAY NINETY

Feel your feelings

Some emotions can be uncomfortable. To avoid facing them, you might push them away, act them out or escape from them via distracting behaviours (tv, social media, etc.) or using substances (e.g. alcohol or drugs).

Your feelings want and need to be felt; they are a communication from your mind. If you notice a feeling, acknowledge it and let it build; notice how it feels in your body. A feeling is not a fact and it can't hurt you. Sit tight until it reaches a point where it peaks. It will then start to subside. Like coming over the top of a hill, relief will come flooding in.

It can take courage and practice, but allow your feelings to come and then let them go.

DAY NINETY ONE

Change your environment

When you're stressed and you don't know how to feel better, another way to shift is to change the environment you're in.

Go outside, or just move into a different room, open the window and breathe some fresh air.

You could try rearranging the furniture and notice what feeling that brings.

As the old saying goes, 'a change is as good as a rest!'

Your body and mood can shift so quickly.

Shake things up and help bring that change!

DAY NINETY TWO
Massage

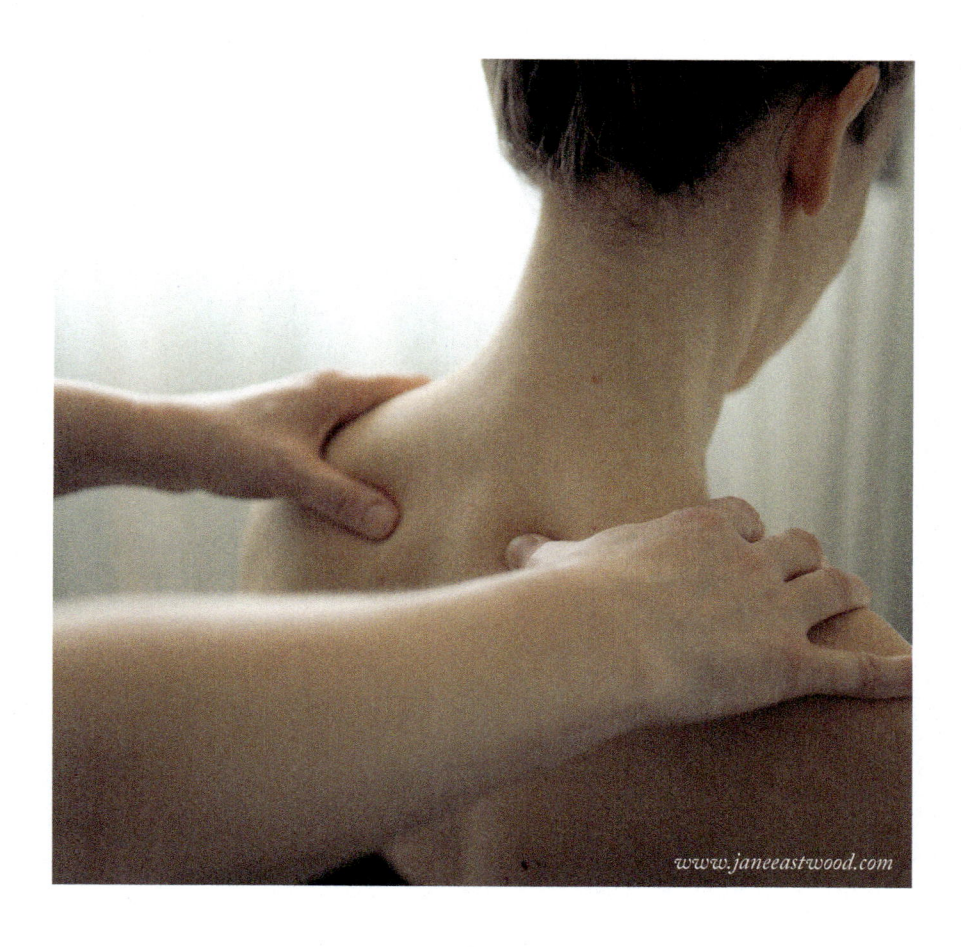

Massage is so good for your body and mind.

Receiving care from another person will help you to let go of stress, as well as soothing and releasing aches and pains in your body.

Whether you book in with a professional, ask a friend or even massage yourself, you will benefit from the skin-to-skin contact.

Sometimes you might not be aware of how tense you are until you start to let go. Just a few minutes' massage can make such a difference and will be a really positive part of your regular self-care routine.

DAY NINETY THREE
Having a fixed outcome

A big cause of stress can be attachment to a fixed outcome; in other words, you will only be happy if things turn out a certain way.

Imagine you are planning the perfect summer picnic; you spend days researching the ideal location, inviting people, preparing the food, packing the picnic basket… and on the day, it pours with rain.

How will you react?
Do you go with it and dance in the rain, or feel disappointed and hard done by?

If you can release some of the expectation and just allow things to unfold, you will find both the journey and the outcome more enjoyable.

Who knows what joy you might discover along the way?

DAY NINETY FOUR
Notice your triggers

A trigger is an occurrence that can set off a reaction; for instance, your alarm clock goes off and you wake up. Some triggers are painful and cause stress, anxiety or even panic attacks, phobias being a prime example.

Do you know what your triggers are?

Deadlines, people, thoughts, road users… a trigger is usually an external influence, but your own thoughts can also ignite negative reactions.

The next time you feel tense, trace the feeling back to the moment it started, which might be a tiny, seemingly insignificant moment. If it wasn't acknowledged at the time, it could start to build, and what began as a minor irritation could grow into a blazing row three days later.

Pay attention to your triggers and release them as they arise.

DAY NINETY FIVE
Affirmations

Affirmations are phrases or words that reinforce a feeling or belief.

A negative affirmation would be: I am not good enough
A positive affirmation would be: I am good enough

Create affirmations that you can use often to help you feel good.

They need to be positive, believable and easy if they are to be successful. Your body will give you feedback on how you feel and whether you really believe what you're saying. Say the phrase out loud and notice how you feel - is it true?

When you have a few affirmations that feel good, carry them with you. Have a note of them in your phone, put them in your wallet, on the fridge or by your bed; having as many reminders as you can of the good things you feel about yourself will help embed them into your subconscious mind.

DAY NINETY SIX
The miracle question

If you could wave a magic wand, and wake up tomorrow to find all your problems were solved, what would be different?

What would you see, hear and feel in this new reality?

Looking at the world with this new perspective can help you feel more motivated and can inspire new ideas.

Maybe you are closer than you think to the stress-free life you really want.

Focus on one area of your life at a time: relationships, health, work, money, fun, your environment, community - what changes would you like to make?

DAY NINETY SEVEN

What is your 'why'?

In these last few days of the 100 Stress-Free Days, it would be wonderful for you to achieve a concrete goal.

When you have settled on your goal, ask yourself why you want it.
What difference will it make to you and others?
How will it feel once you have achieved it?

Knowing WHY you are heading towards that objective will inspire you, and is key to keeping you motivated. You probably want something because of the feeling it will bring you.

Do you dream of a pain-free, healthy body, for example?
Working towards this end goal will help you make good choices along the way, and make the end result all the sweeter.

DAY NINETY EIGHT
Commit

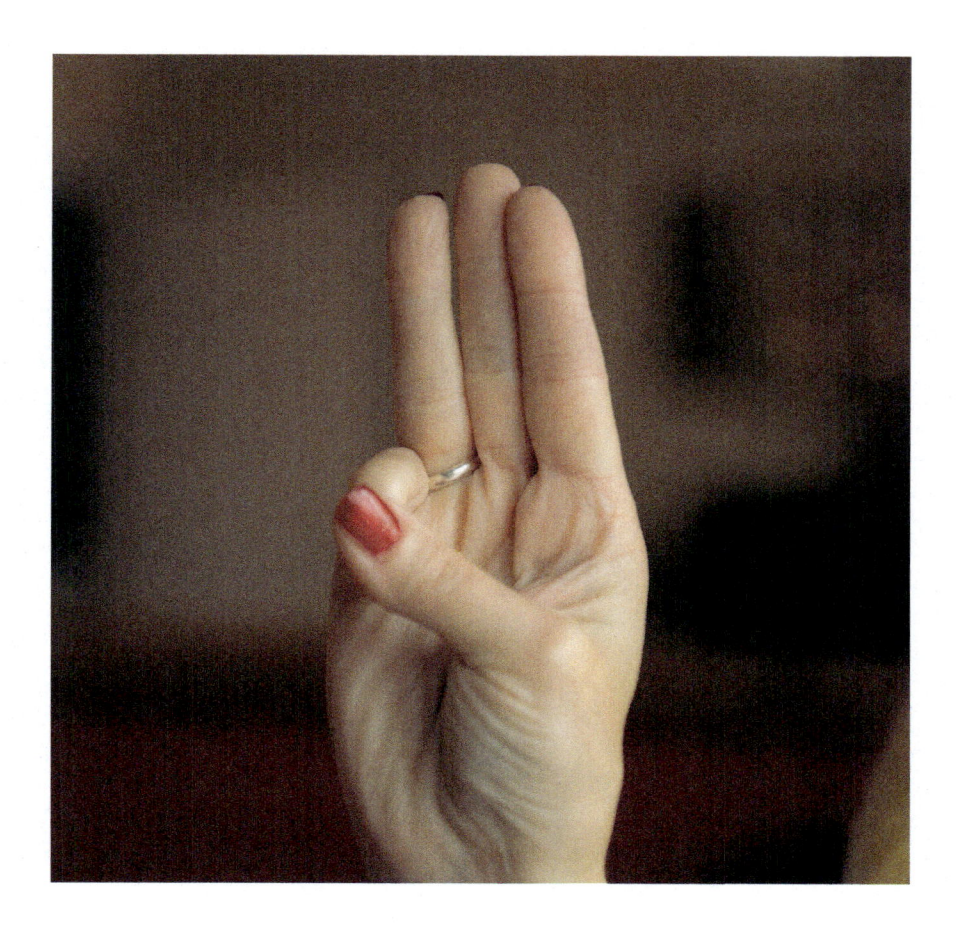

Following on from yesterday, you've now set a goal. You know why you want it, how it's going to make you feel and you're making it happen.

The next step is to commit to the process; that means marking in your diary the date you're going to start or finish.

Making a commitment to yourself will help you reinforce your decision. Try writing yourself a declaration, signing it and putting it somewhere you can see it often.

What you want isn't going to fall in your lap, but sending yourself a clear message will help you feel determined to attain it.

Your commitment shows your value and ambition; keep your promise to yourself and feel proud of what you can achieve.

DAY NINETY NINE
Accountability

Accountability is like super-charging your commitment.

Over the last few days, you've set a goal, you know why you're doing it and you're committed. When you talk about what you want you begin to create it.

When you're accountable to someone else, you are much more likely to attain your goal. Choose wisely; the best person is someone who will check in with you, remind you and keep you on track.

Tell them what you want to achieve, when and why you're doing it, and your next steps. Ask them to walk by your side and cheerlead you to success.

When life takes over, our dreams can take a back seat - accountability won't let that happen.

DAY ONE HUNDRED
Celebrate!

You did it. Day 100!

Celebrating your achievements is so important.

Acknowledging how far you've travelled and the struggles you've overcome along the way will fix what you've learnt, build your self-confidence - and feel amazing!

Make sure you celebrate when you start something, as often as you can along the way and at the end of your journey. Share the joy and be an inspiration to those around you.

What will you celebrate today?

NOTES

Day One - Breathe

Day Two - Tap One Round of EFT

Day Three - Pivoting - Choose the opposite

Day Four - Go for a walk

Day Five - Women's Day - Reach out to a woman in your life

Day Six - Tidy one area

Day Seven - If you need help, get help

Day Eight - Meditation

Day Nine - Set your intention

Day Ten - Finishing things - your to-do list

Day Eleven - Connect with someone

Day Twelve - Tap in the positive

Day Thirteen - Tune!

Day Fourteen - Take a different view

Day Fifteen - Try hypnotherapy

Day Sixteen - Do nothing for 5 minutes

Day Seventeen - Get creative

Day Eighteen - Mix it up - Do something differently

Day Nineteen - Come up with 10 solutions to a problem

Day Twenty - What's the best advice you've ever been given?

Day Twenty One - Set yourself a health challenge

Day Twenty Two - Focus on what makes you happy

Day Twenty Three - Have compassion

Day Twenty Four - Find a rainbow

Day Twenty Five - Have a bath

Day Twenty Six - Evoke the Learning State

Day Twenty Seven - What's the kindest thing you could say to yourself?

Day Twenty Eight - What advice would you give your younger self?

Day Twenty Nine - Drink more water

Day Thirty - If you had a shop, what would you sell?

Day Thirty One - Walk down a path you've never been down before

Day Thirty Two - List your 10 best qualities

Day Thirty Three - Focus on your future self

Day Thirty Four - Take one tiny step towards your goal

Day Thirty Five - List of all the good things and good people in your life

Day Thirty Six - Describe a happy memory

Day Thirty Seven - Stop pushing - What self-care do you need?

Day Thirty Eight - Emergency tapping

Day Thirty Nine - Get organised

Day Forty - Make a decision

Day Forty One - Your body Language

Day Forty Two - Watch your language

Day Forty Three - Say "no" if it's a "no"

Day Forty Four - Tense and release

Day Forty Five - Write down your worries and three things you are grateful for

Day Forty Six - Good sleep routine

Day Forty Seven - It's OK not to be OK

Day Forty Eight - Procrastination

Day Forty Nine - Overcome overwhelm

Day Fifty - Keep going

Day Fifty One - Choose a word for the day
- Peace

Day Fifty Two - Look around you with fresh eyes

Day Fifty Three - Have a nap

Day Fifty Four - Hot & Cold emotions game

Day Fifty Five - Let the Earth support you

Day Fifty Six - Respond rather than react

Day Fifty Seven - Havening

Day Fifty Eight - Happy buttons

Day Fifty Nine - Heartmath breathing technique

Day Sixty - Trust the process

Day Sixty One - Give yourself a break

Day Sixty Two - Forgive something from your past

Day Sixty Three - List ten things that went well

Day Sixty Four - Eat an apple mindfully

Day Sixty Five - See how far you've come

Day Sixty Six - Comfort break

Day Sixty Seven - Morning Pages

Day Sixty Eight - Loving Kindness Meditation

Day Sixty Nine - White Light Meditation

Day Seventy - Silence

Day Seventy One - Write with your non-dominant hand

Day Seventy Two - Move into the learning zone

Day Seventy Three - What you think is the problem, isn't the problem.

Day Seventy Four - Clear out your old clothes

Day Seventy Five - What would... do

Day Seventy Six - Act as if...

Day Seventy Seven - 4-7-8 Breathing Technique

Day Seventy Eight - Listen to your body

Day Seventy Nine - Count something

Day Eighty - Who needs your help?

Day Eighty One - Exercise

Day Eighty Two - 'Eat the frog'

Day Eighty Three - Go fast go alone, go far go together

Day Eighty Four - Projection

Day Eighty Five - Tap to ground yourself

Day Eighty Six - Laugh!

Day Eighty Seven - Change your thoughts

Day Eighty Eight - Plan a surprise for someone

Day Eighty Nine - Don't put it off

Day Ninety - Feel your feelings

Day Ninety One - Change your environment

Day Ninety Two - Massage

Day Ninety Three - Having a fixed outcome

Day Ninety Four - Notice your triggers

Day Ninety Five - Affirmations

Day Ninety Six - The miracle question

Day Ninety Seven - What is your 'why'?

Day Ninety Eight - Commitment

Day Ninety Nine - Accountability

Day One Hundred - Celebrate

Thank you!!!

It's been such a joy and a privilege to share these tips with you. I would love to hear your favourite!

Send me an email to jemima@stressfreelifeacademy.com

or post to instagram

#100stressfreedays @stressfreelifeacademy

www.stressfreelifeacademy.com

Printed in Great Britain
by Amazon